cocktail jazz

Arranged by Brent Edstrom

contents

ISBN 978-1-4950-6894-2

7777 W. BLUEMOUND RD. P.O. BOX 13819 MILWAUKEE, WI 53213

Visit Hal Leonard Online at
www.halleonard.com

ALFIE
Theme from the Paramount Picture ALFIE

Words by HAL DAVID
Music by BURT BACHARACH

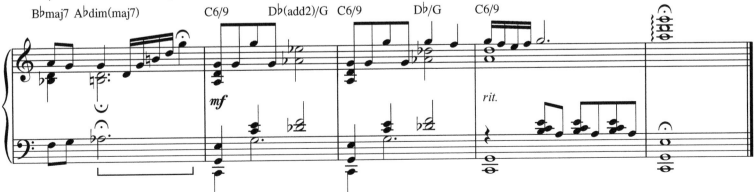

ALL THE WAY

from THE JOKER IS WILD

Words by SAMMY CAHN
Music by JAMES VAN HEUSEN

Flowing Ballad

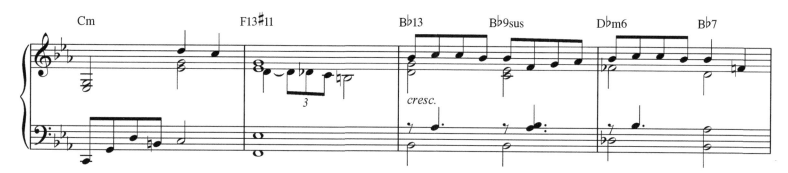

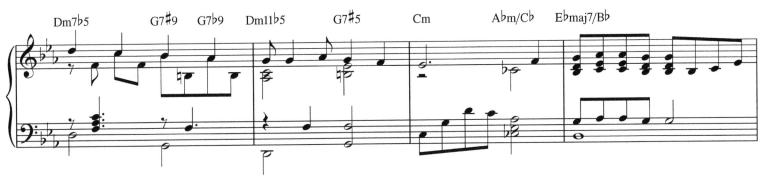

Relaxed Swing

6

Swing 16ths

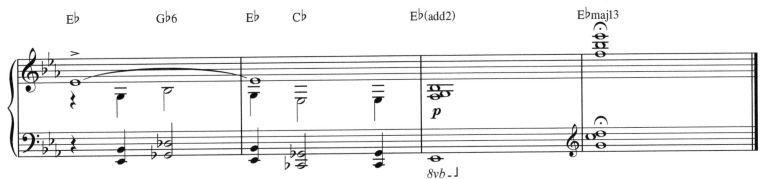

AS TIME GOES BY

from CASABLANCA

Words and Music by
HERMAN HUPFELD

Moderately slow, freely

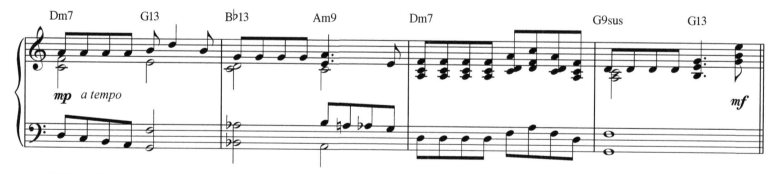

Lilting Swing

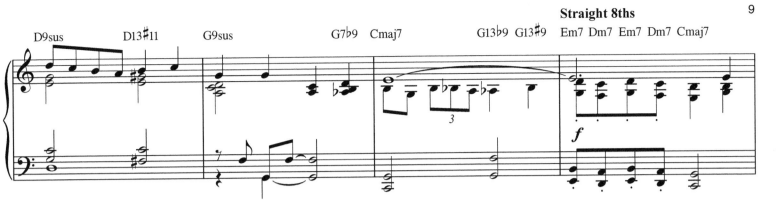

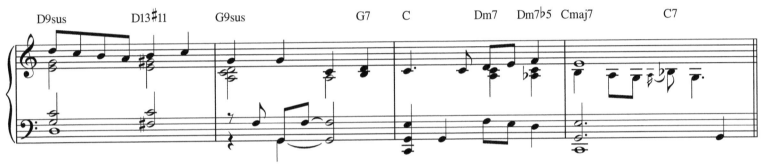

To Coda ⊕

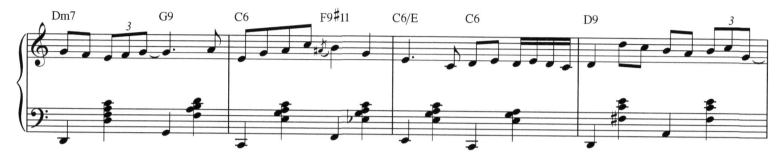

D.S. al Coda

CODA

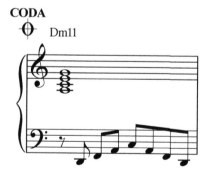

8vb

CHARADE
from CHARADE

Music by HENRY MANCINI
Words by JOHNNY MERCER

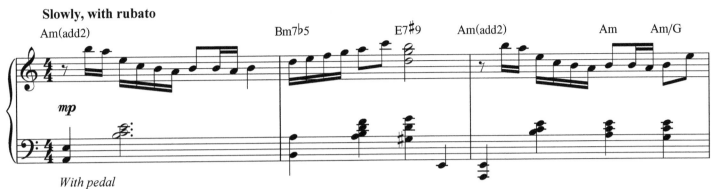

Slowly, with rubato

Flowing, slightly more motion

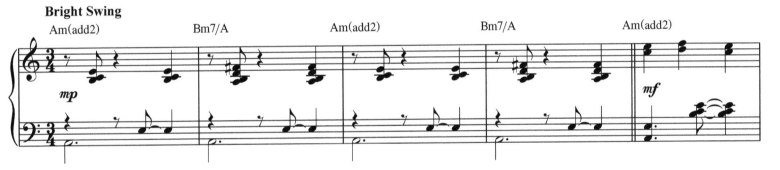

Bright Swing

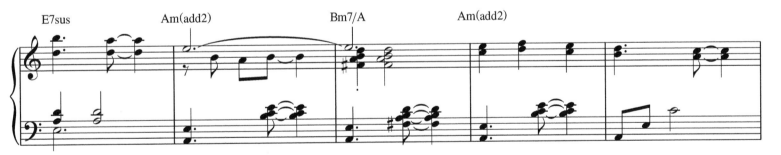

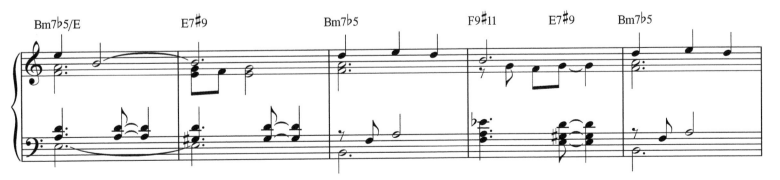

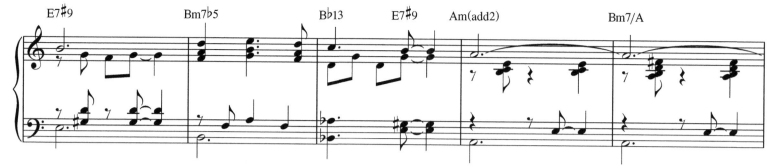

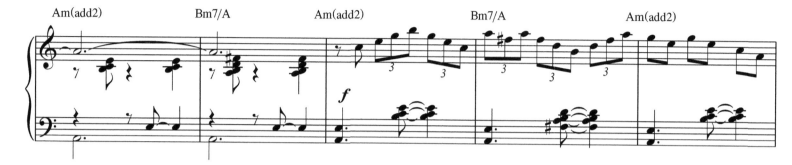

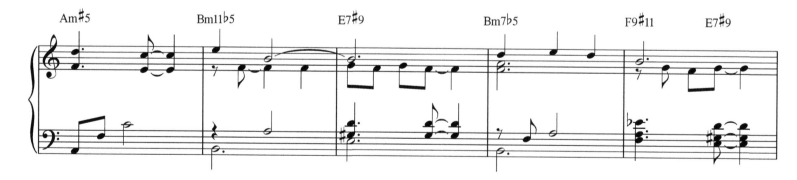

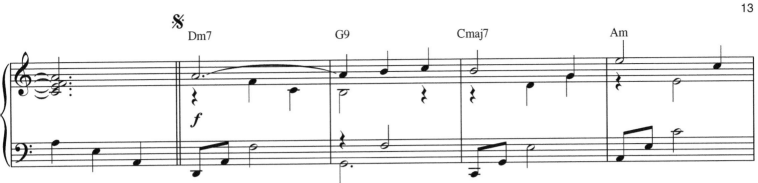

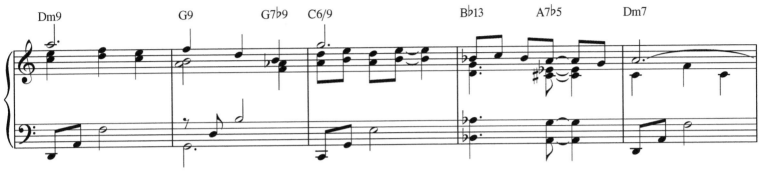

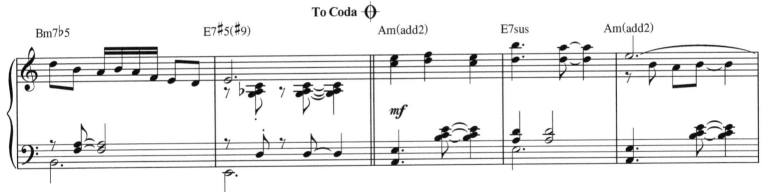

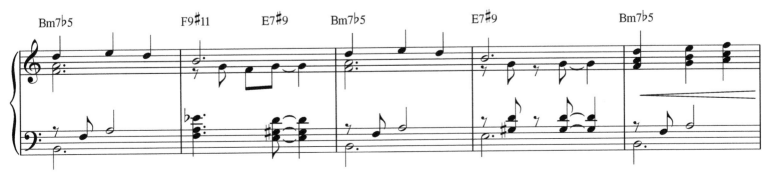

14

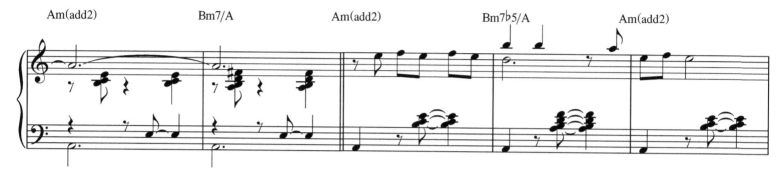

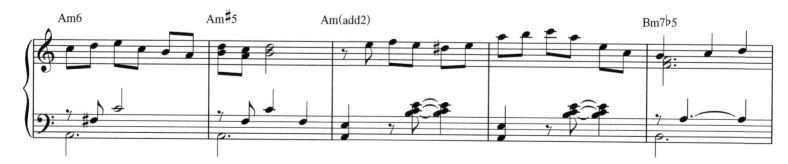

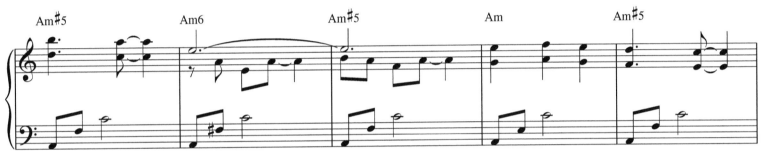

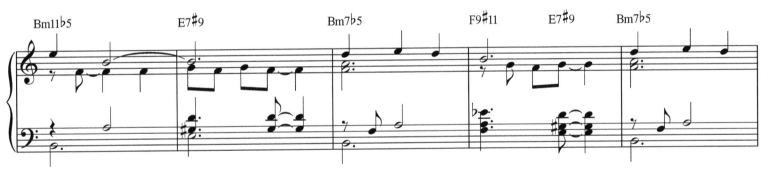

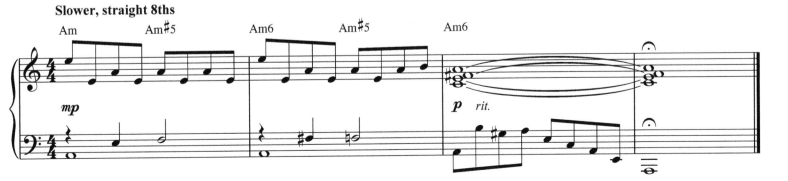

AUTUMN IN NEW YORK

Words and Music by
VERNON DUKE

Slowly, poco rubato

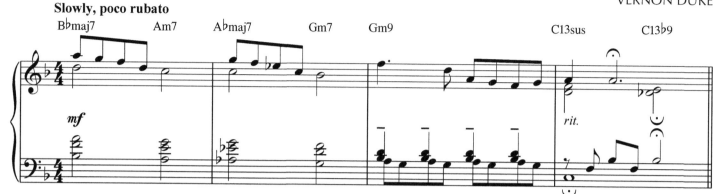

Steady Ballad tempo

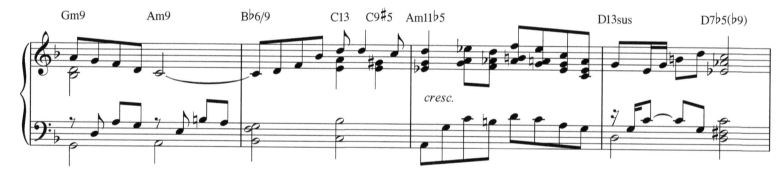

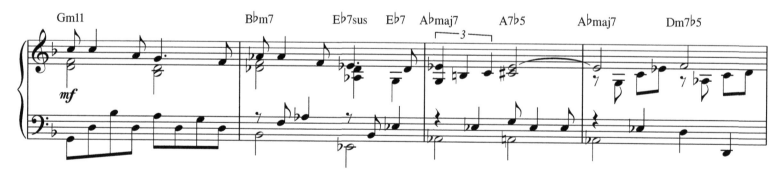

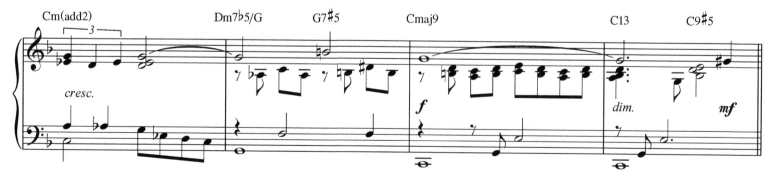

BLAME IT ON MY YOUTH

Words by EDWARD HEYMAN
Music by OSCAR LEVANT

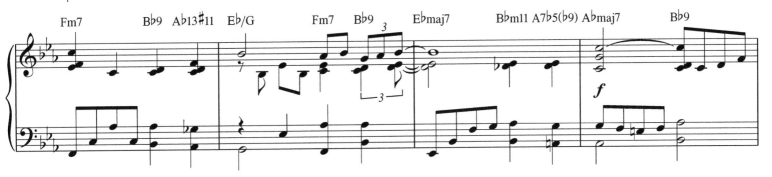

COME FLY WITH ME

Words by SAMMY CAHN
Music by JAMES VAN HEUSEN

Moderately slow, straight 8ths

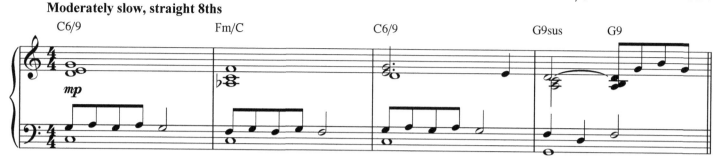

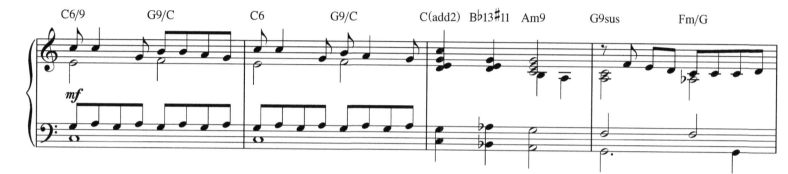

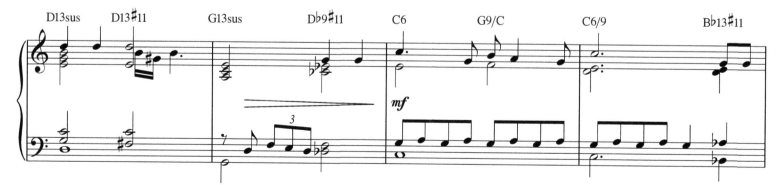

Moderate Swing

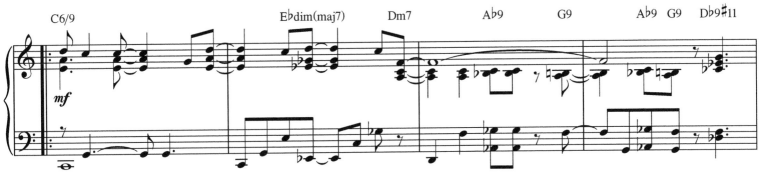

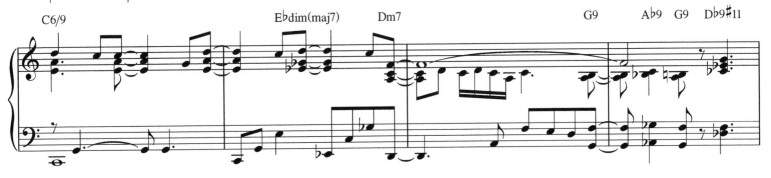

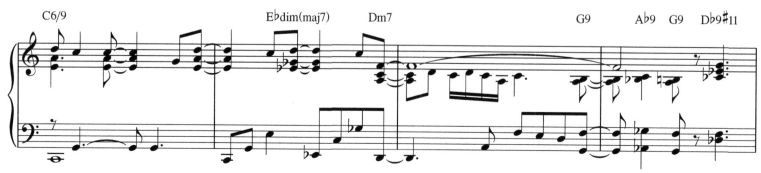

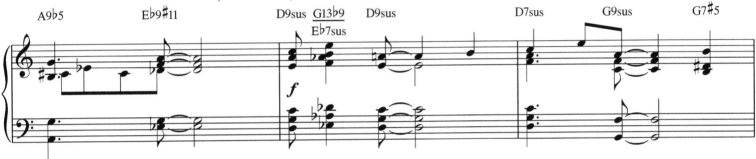

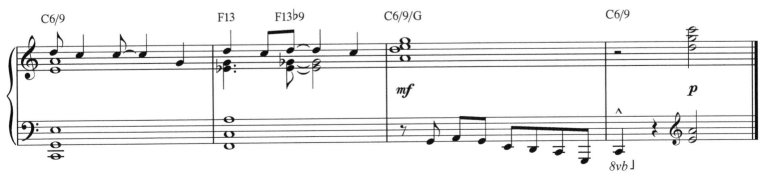

CUTE

Music by NEAL HEFTI
Words by STANLEY STYNE

Medium Swing

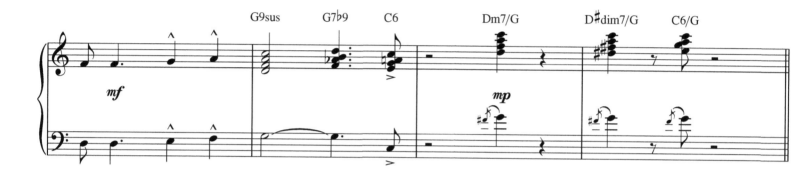

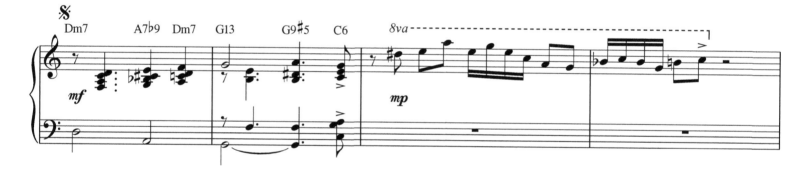

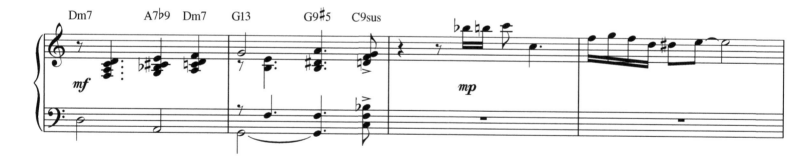

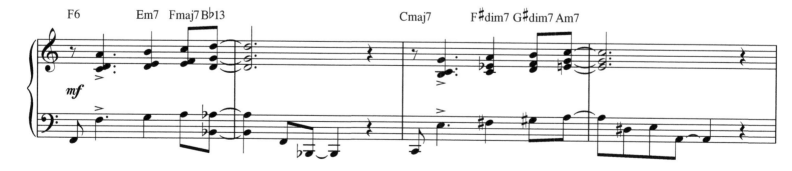

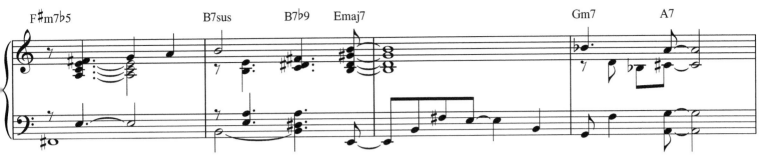

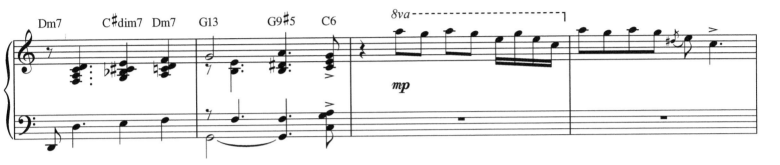

To Coda ⊕

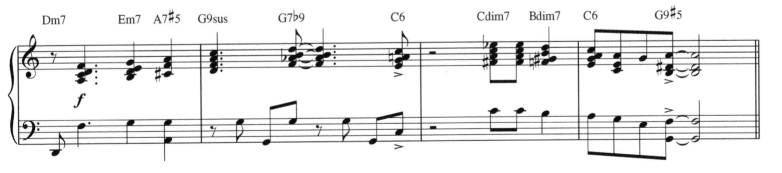

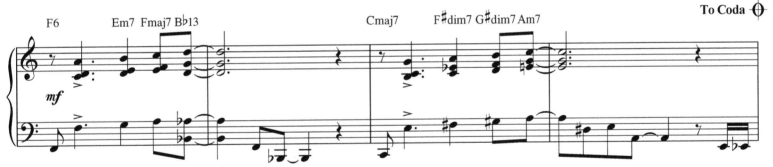

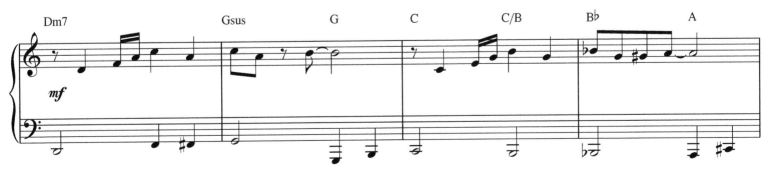

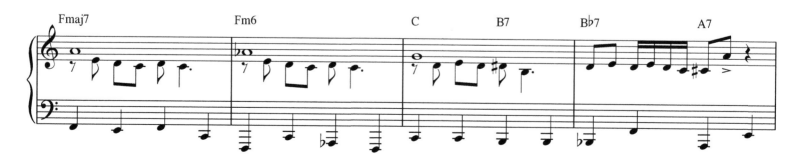

Double-time feel

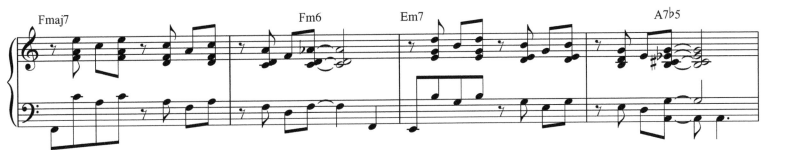

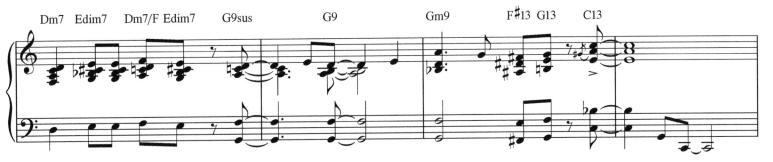

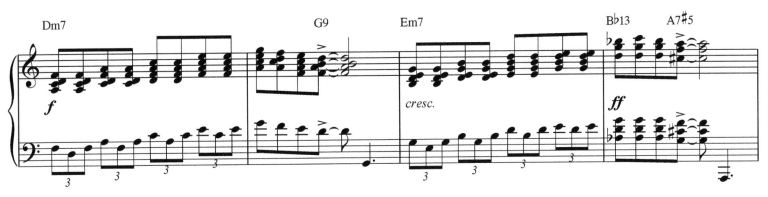

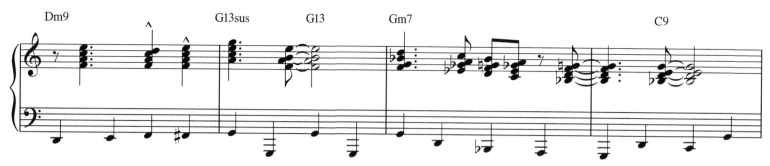

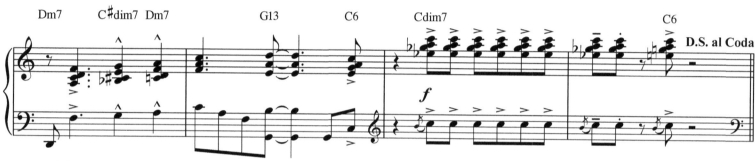

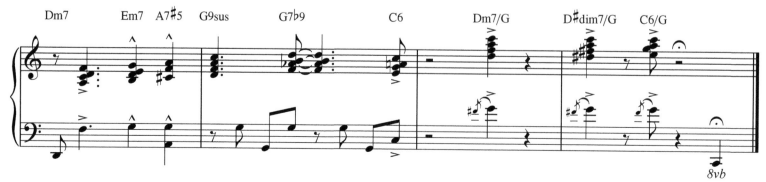

8vb

I'LL BE SEEING YOU

from RIGHT THIS WAY

Written by IRVING KAHAL
and SAMMY FAIN

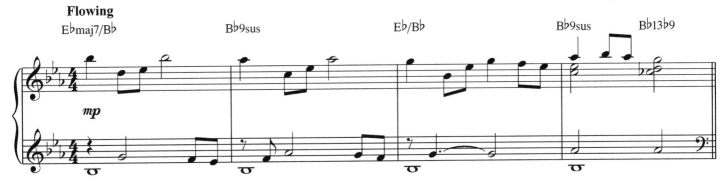

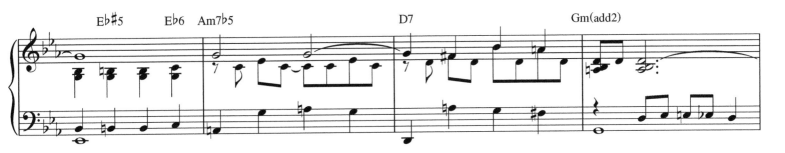

Slow Swing

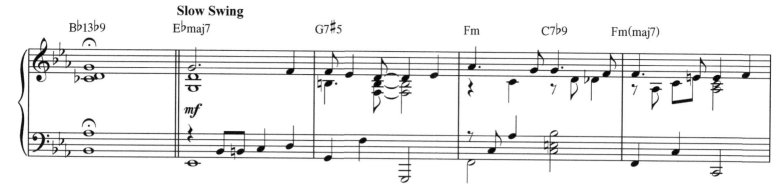

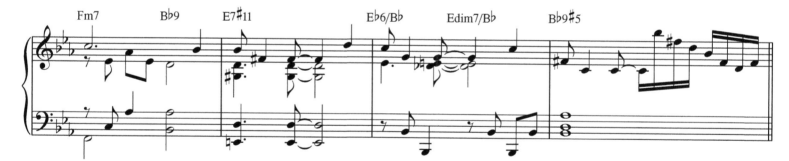

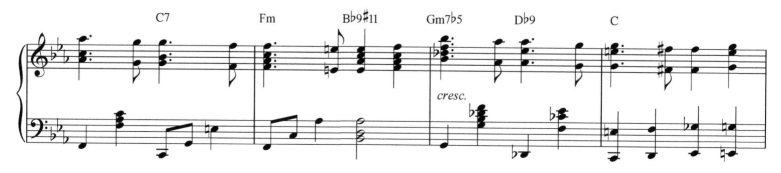

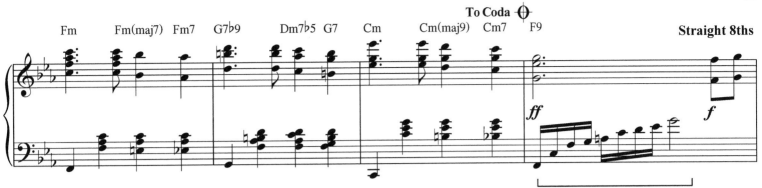

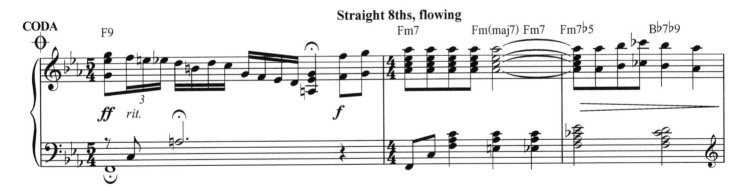

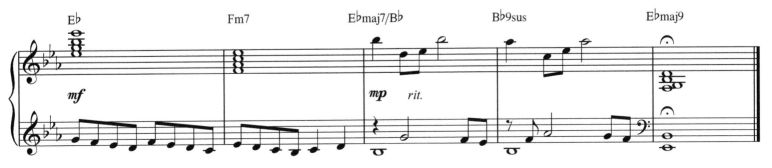

DAYS OF WINE AND ROSES

from DAYS OF WINE AND ROSES

Lyrics by JOHNNY MERCER
Music by HENRY MANCINI

Moderately slow Bossa

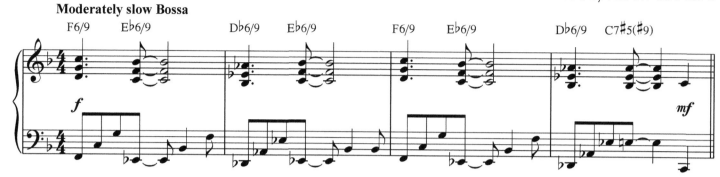

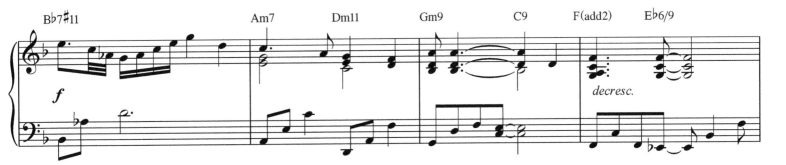

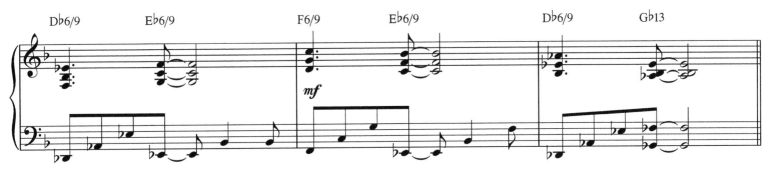

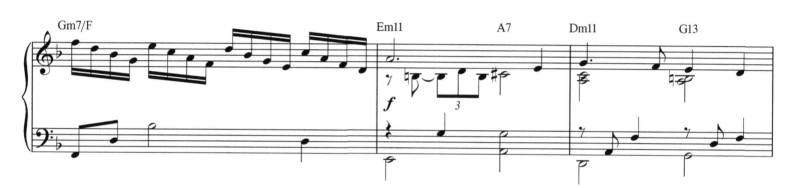

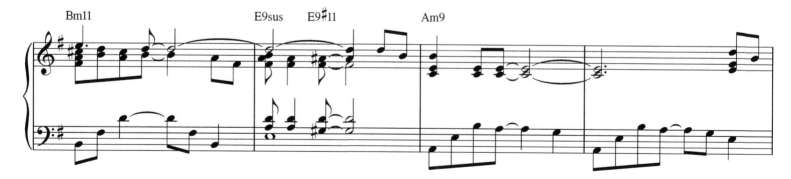

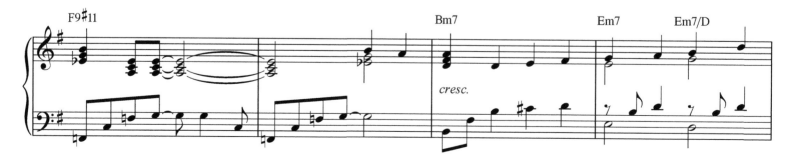

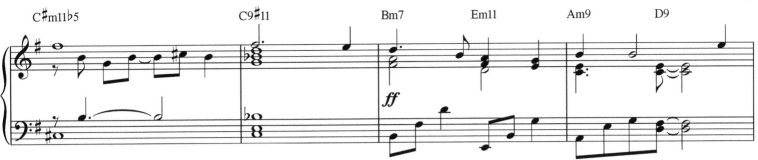

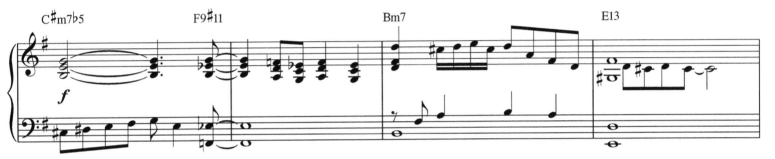

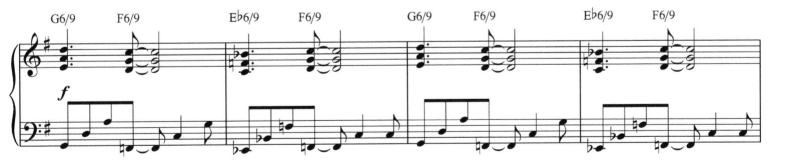

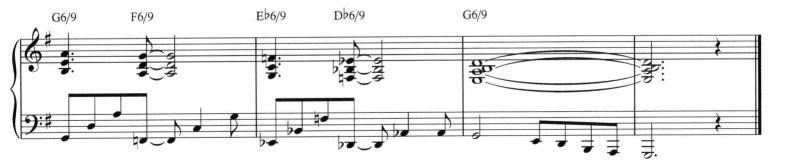

DREAM

Words and Music by
JOHNNY MERCER

Slowly, with expression, straight 8ths

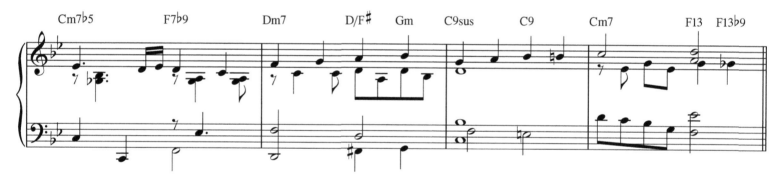

Relaxed Swing

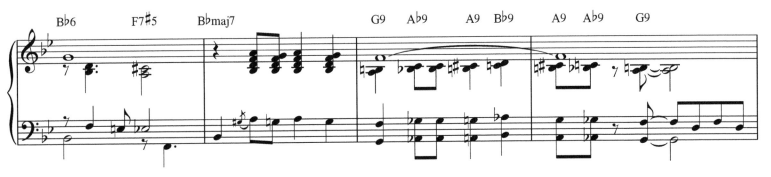

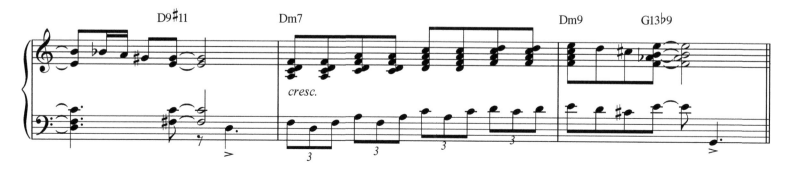

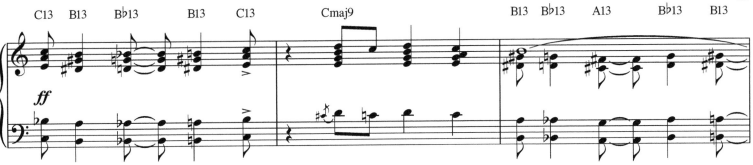

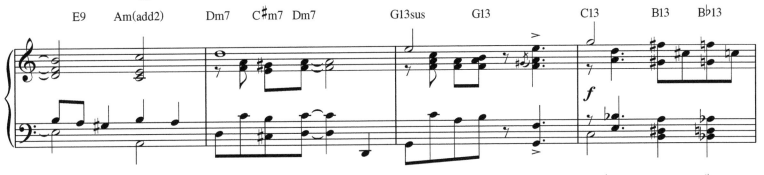

EASY LIVING
Theme from the Paramount Picture EASY LIVING

Words and Music by LEO ROBIN
and RALPH RAINGER

Freely

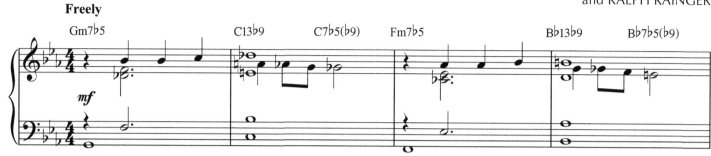

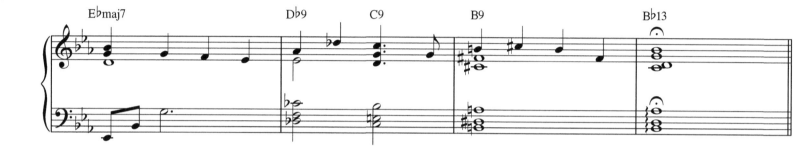

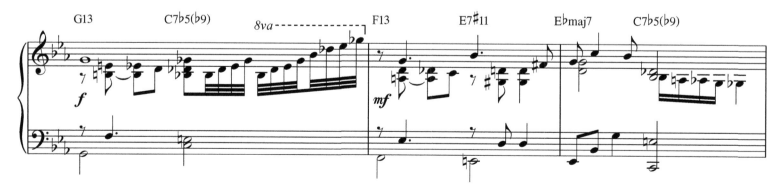

Easy Swing

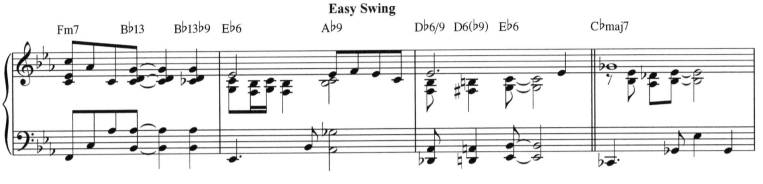

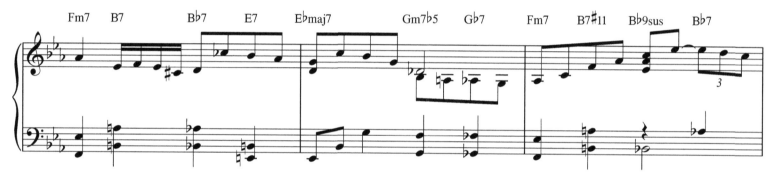

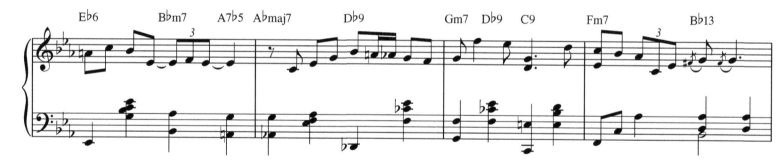

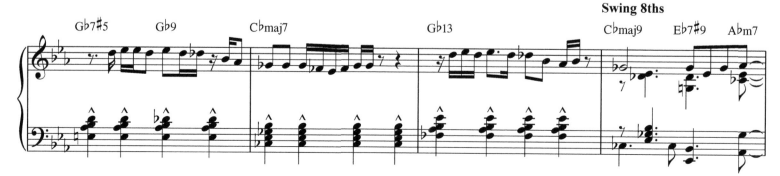

I GET A KICK OUT OF YOU

from ANYTHING GOES

Words and Music by
COLE PORTER

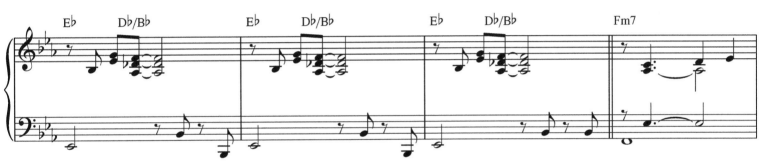

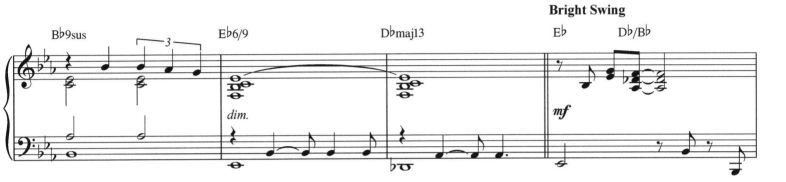

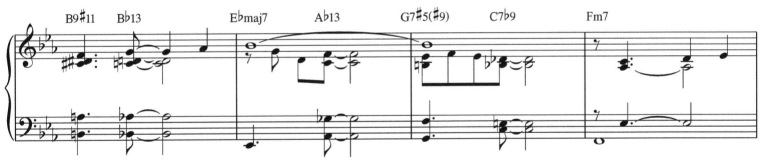

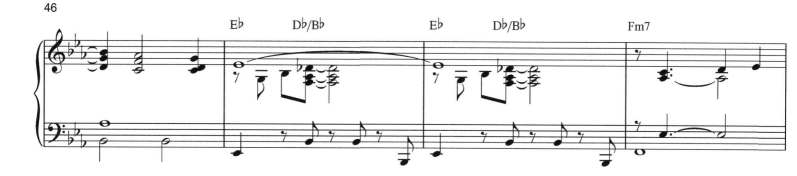

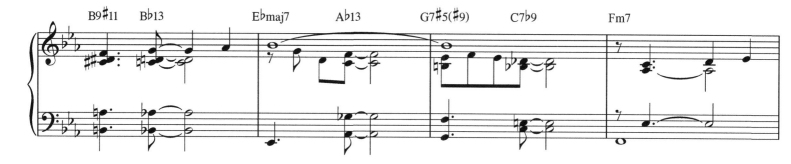

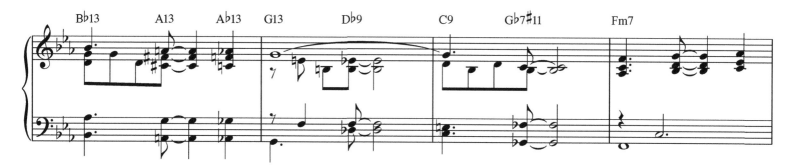

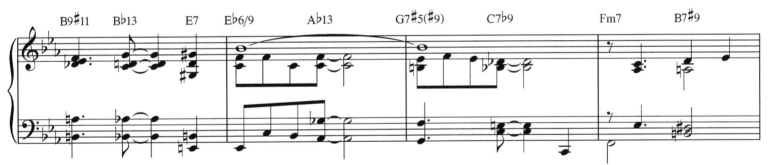

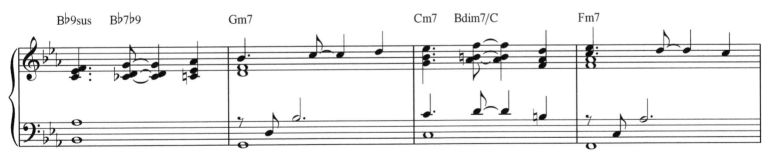

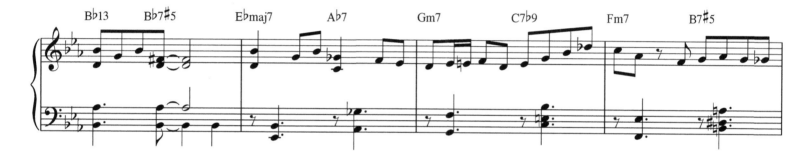

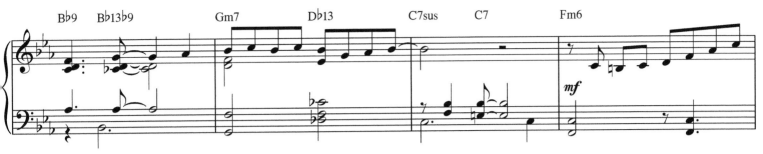

I'VE GOT THE WORLD ON A STRING

Words by TED KOEHLER
Music by HAROLD ARLEN

Medium Swing

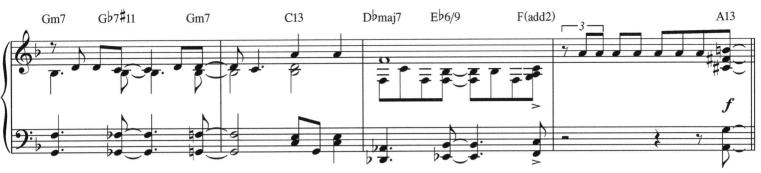

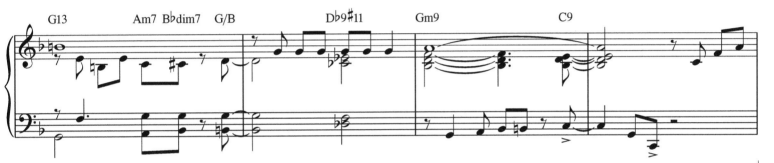

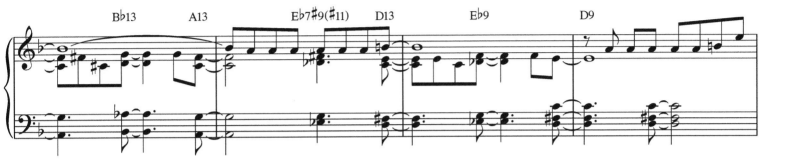

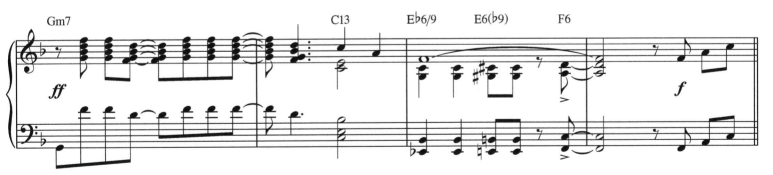

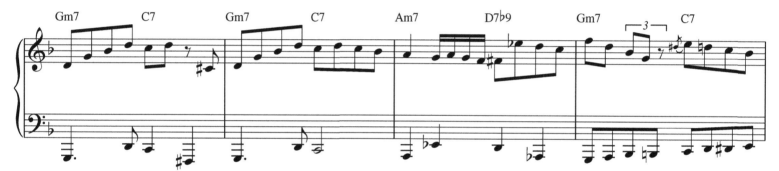

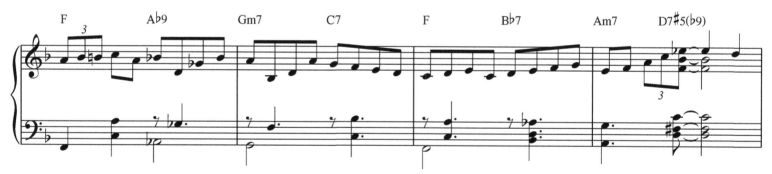

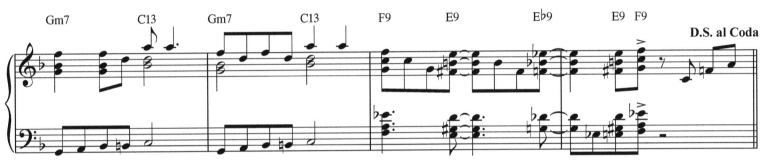

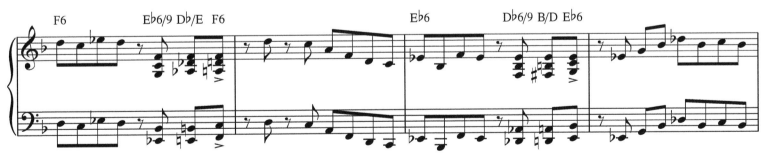

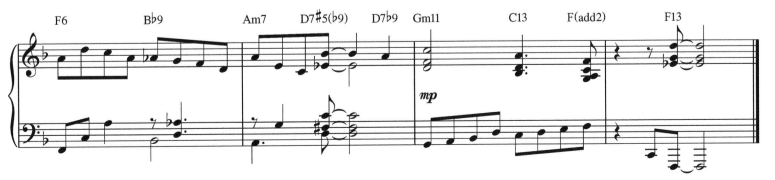

IF HE WALKED INTO MY LIFE

from MAME

Music and Lyric by
JERRY HERMAN

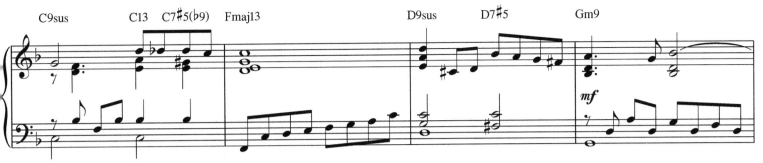

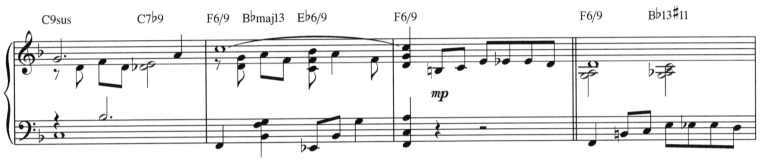

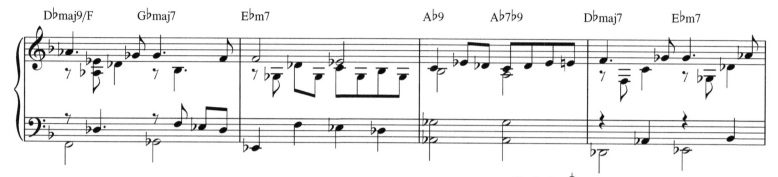

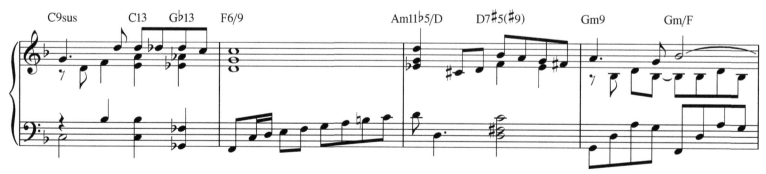

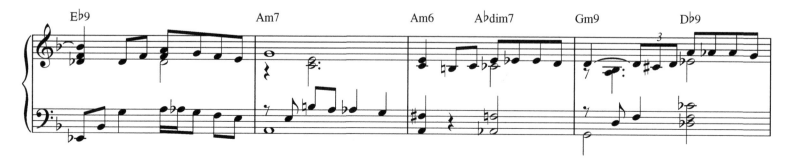

Double-time feel, Swing 16ths

Swing 8ths

Swing 16ths

Swing 8ths

D.S. al Coda

CODA

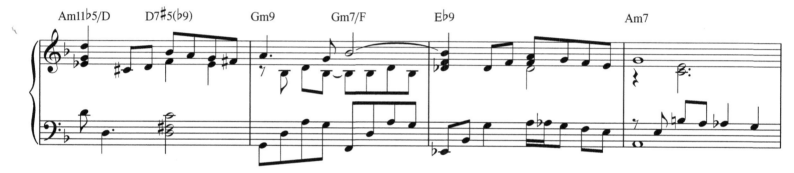

ISN'T IT A PITY?

from PARDON MY ENGLISH

Music and Lyrics by GEORGE GERSHWIN
and IRA GERSHWIN

Flowing, with rubato

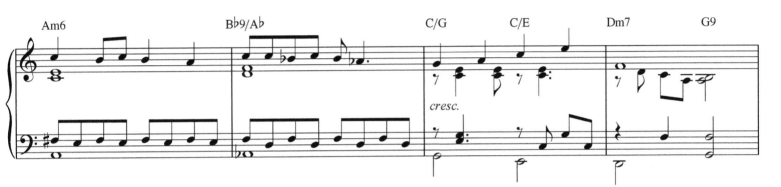

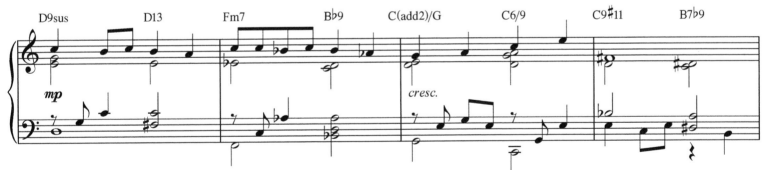

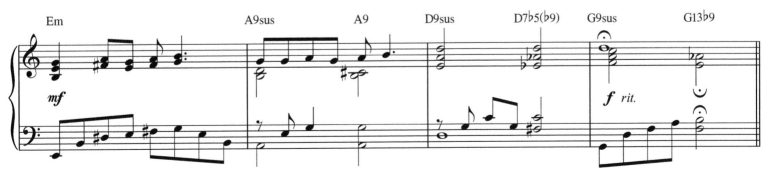

Steady Swing, not too fast

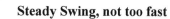

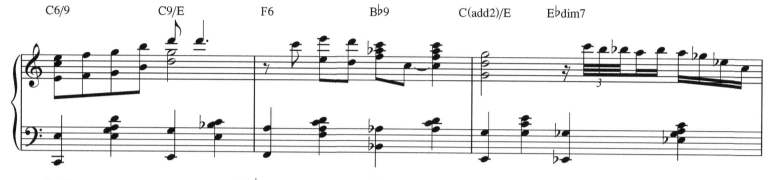
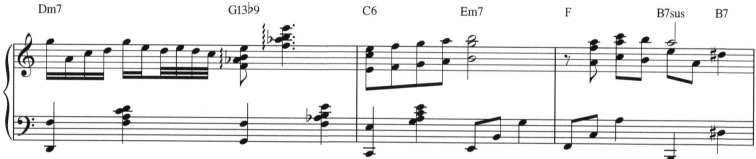
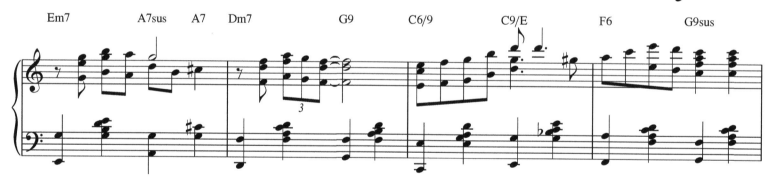
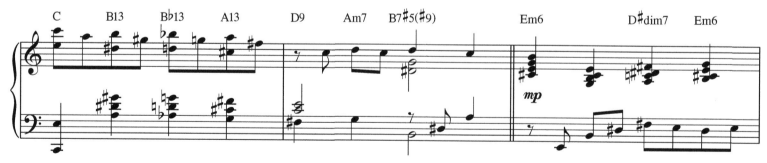

IT COULD HAPPEN TO YOU
from the Paramount Picture AND THE ANGELS SING

Words by JOHNNY BURKE
Music by JAMES VAN HEUSEN

Slowly, with expression

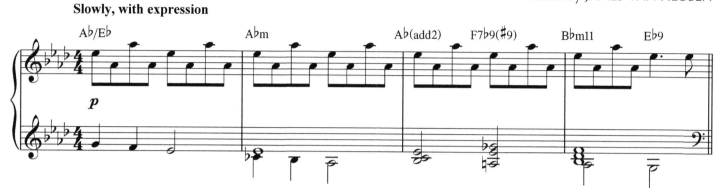

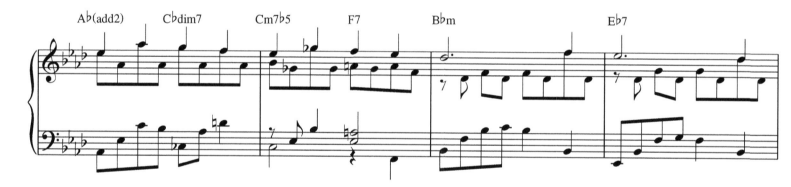

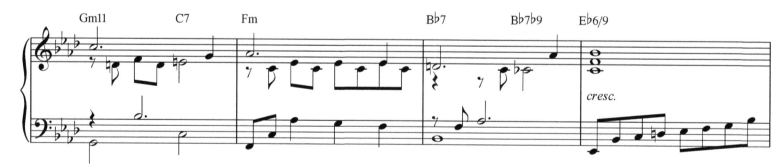

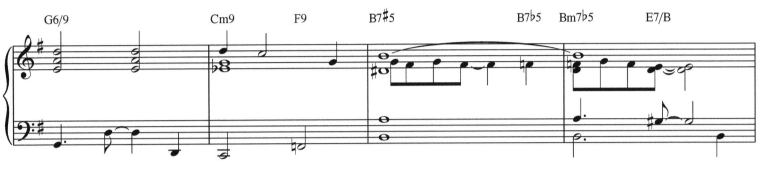

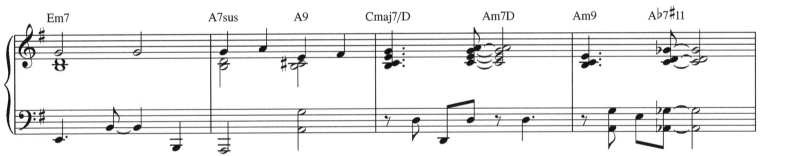

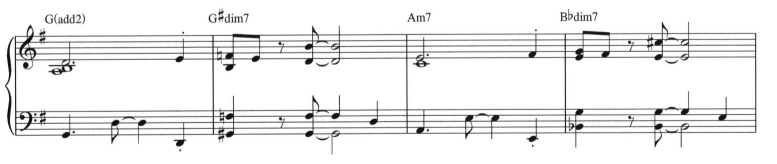

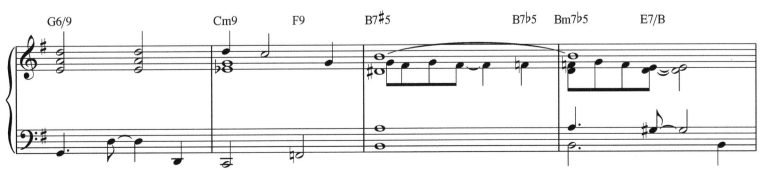

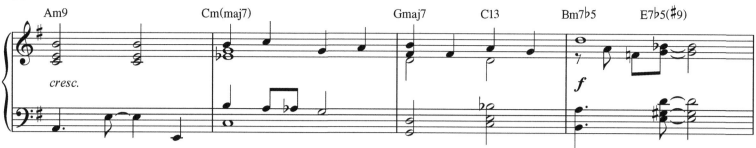

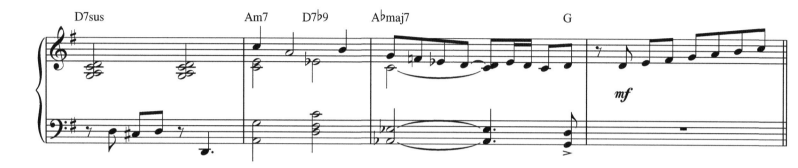

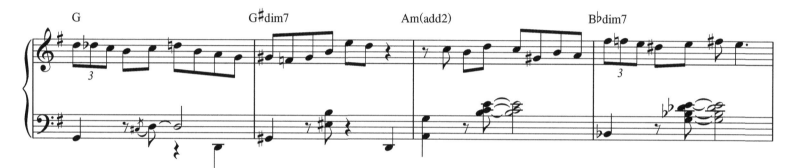

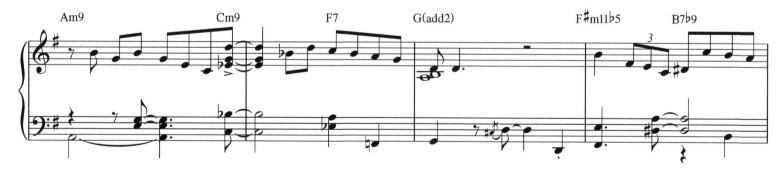

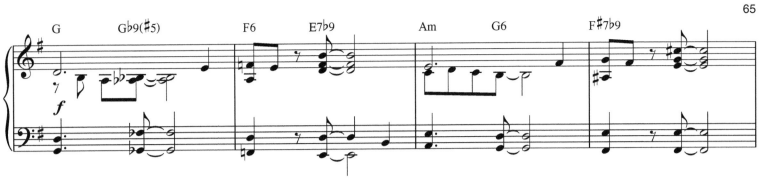

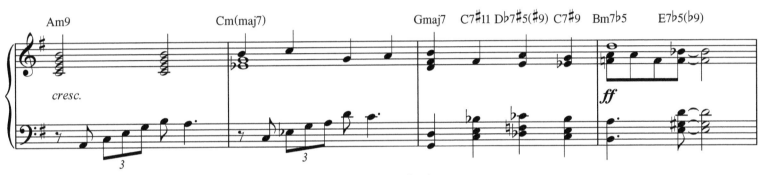

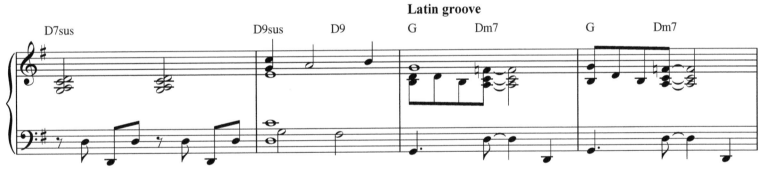

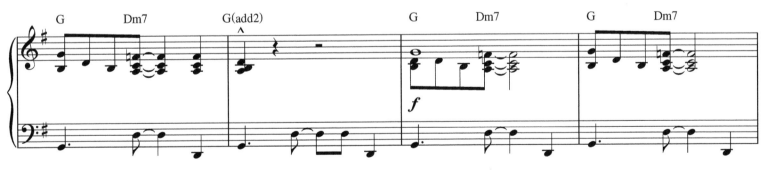

IT HAD TO BE YOU

Words by GUS KAHN
Music by ISHAM JONES

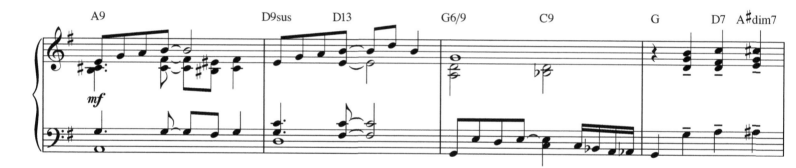

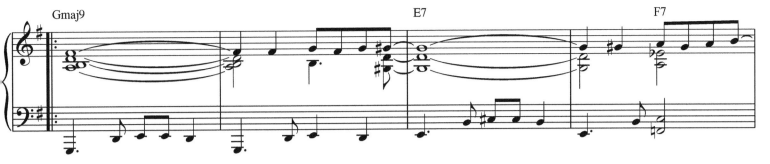

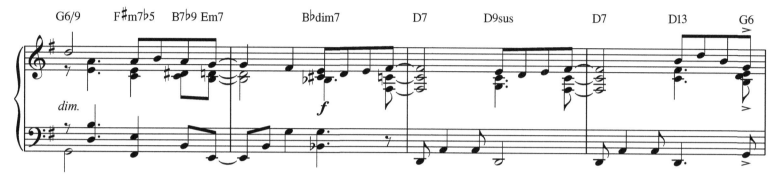

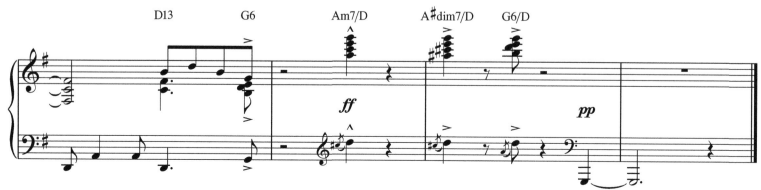

SCOTCH AND SODA

Words and Music by
DAVE GUARD

Moderately slow Blues

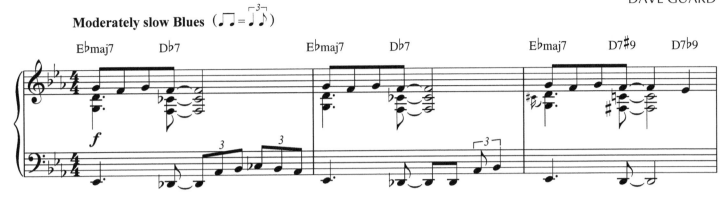

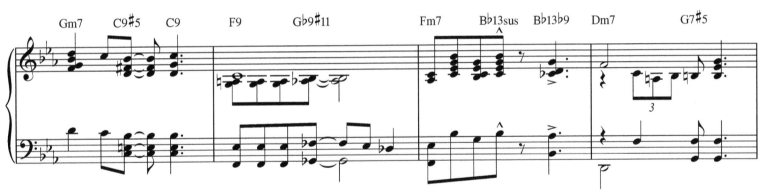

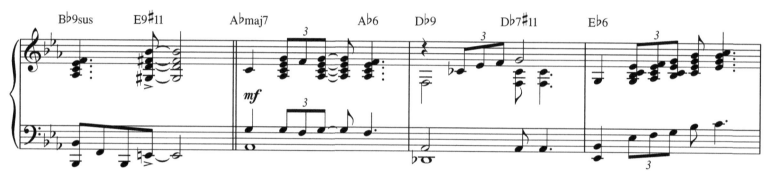

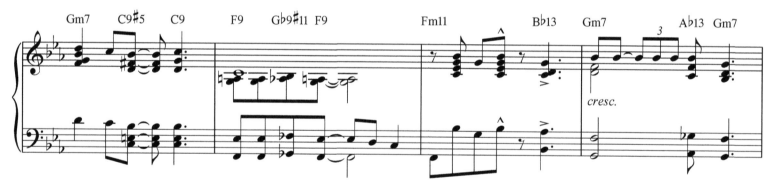

Double-time feel **Swing 16ths**

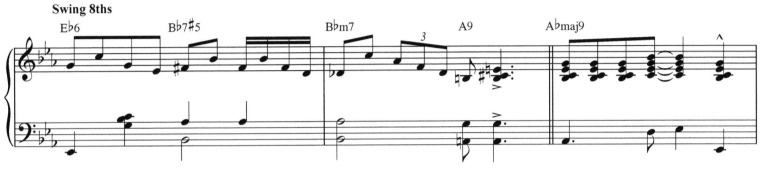

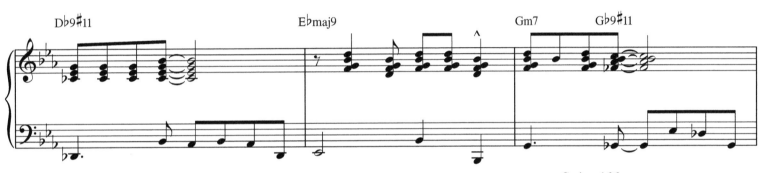

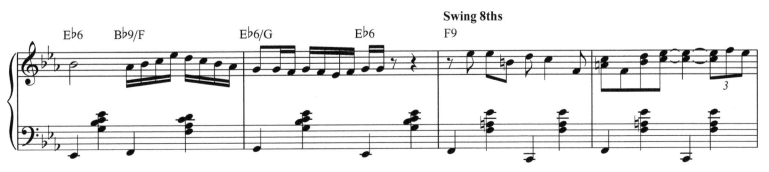

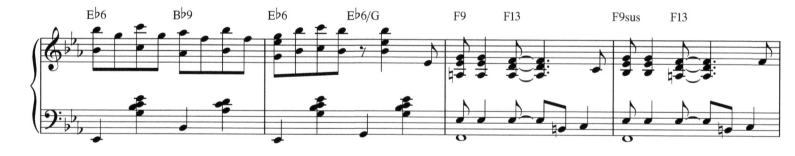

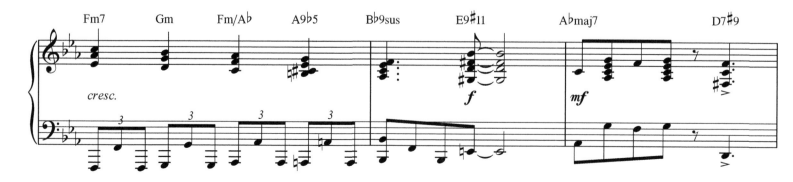

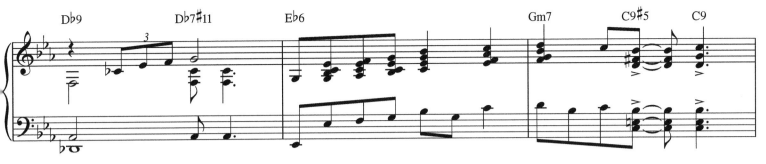

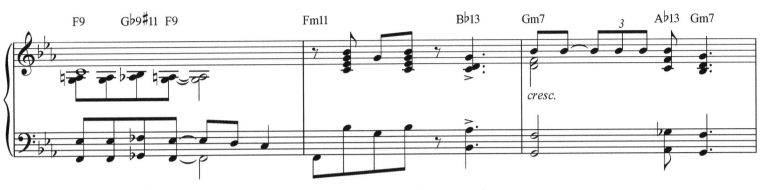

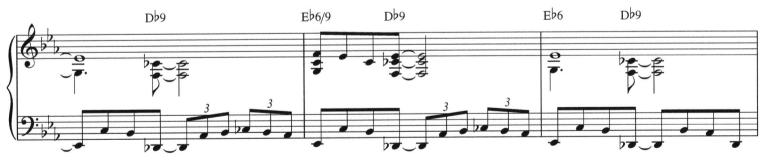

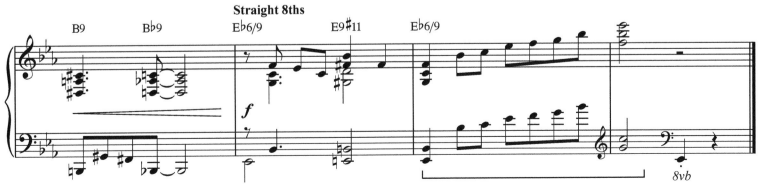

MEDITATION
(Meditacão)

Music by ANTONIO CARLOS JOBIM
Original Words by NEWTON MENDONÇA
English Words by NORMAN GIMBEL

Relaxed Bossa Nova

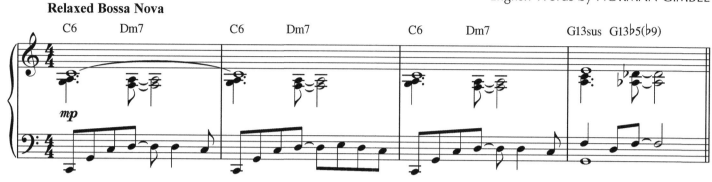

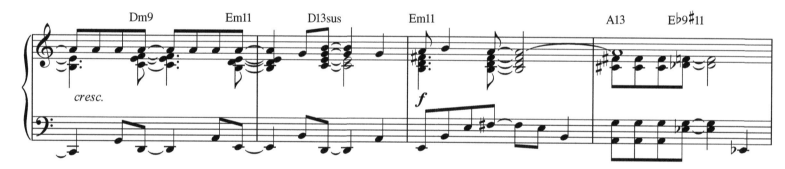

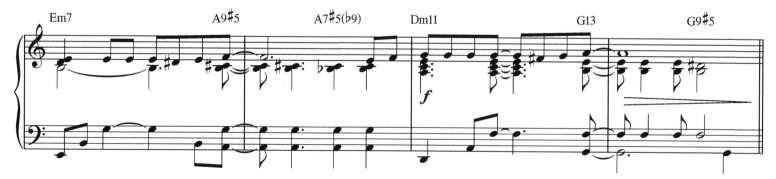

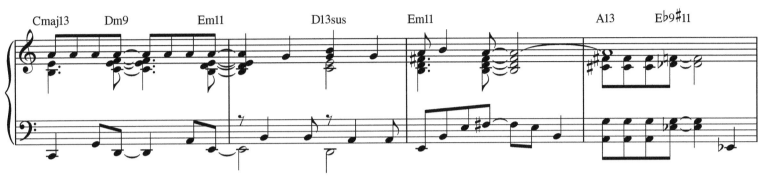

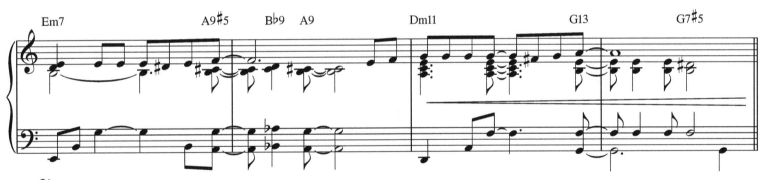

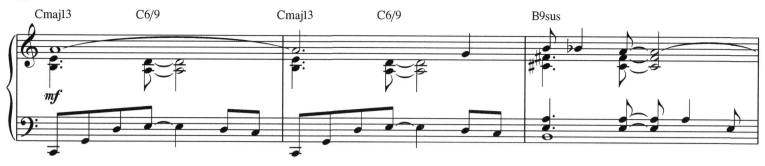

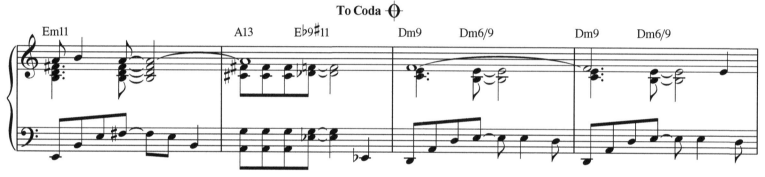

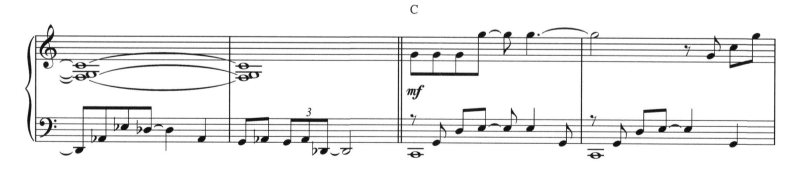

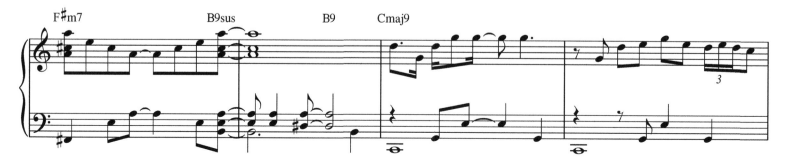

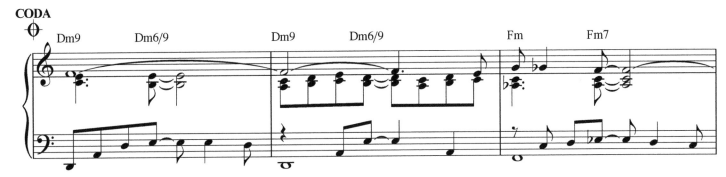

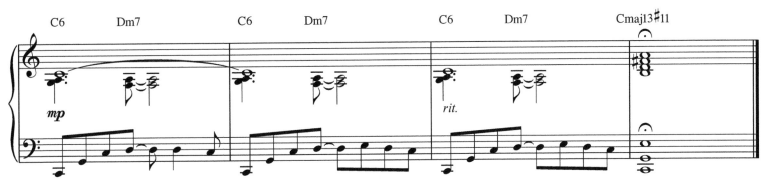

NANCY WITH THE LAUGHING FACE

Words by PHIL SILVERS
Music by JAMES VAN HEUSEN

Moderate Swing

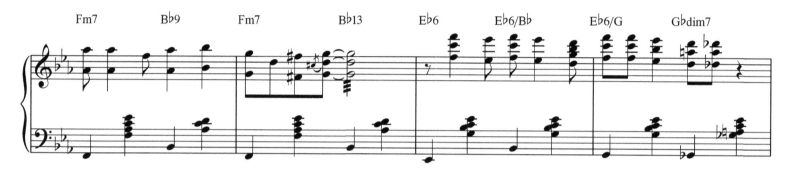

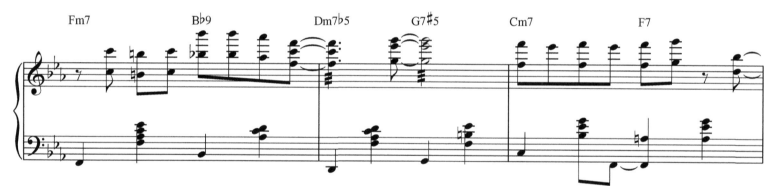

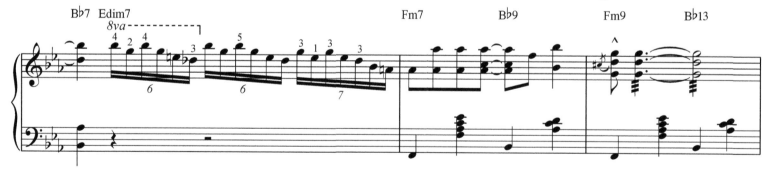

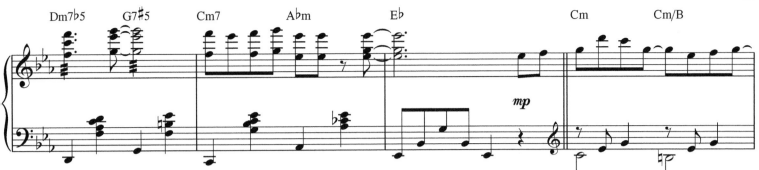

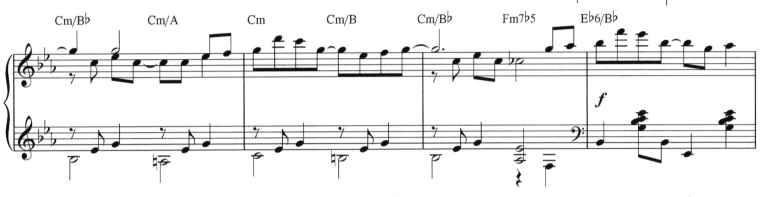

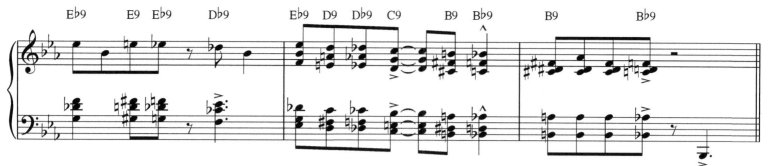

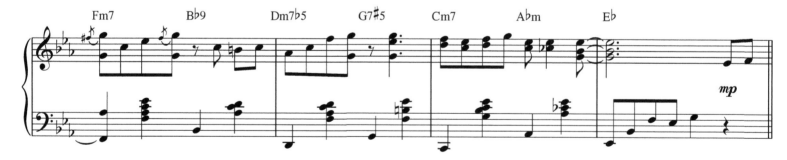

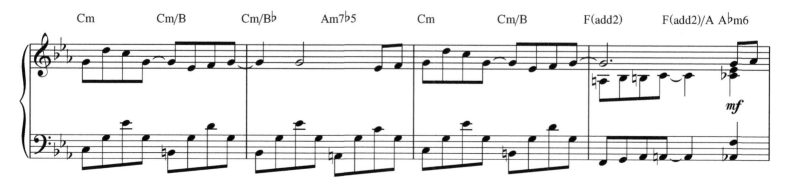

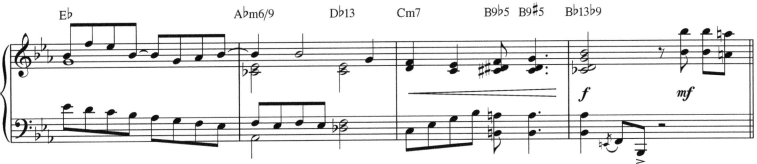

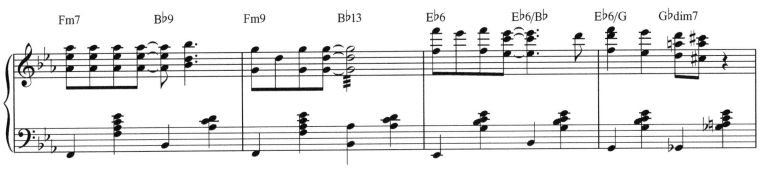

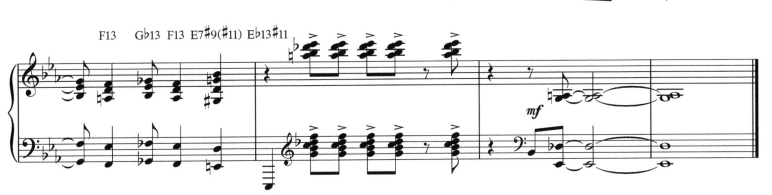

NEVER NEVER LAND

from PETER PAN

Lyric by BETTY COMDEN and ADOLPH GREEN
Music by JULE STYNE

Moderate Swing

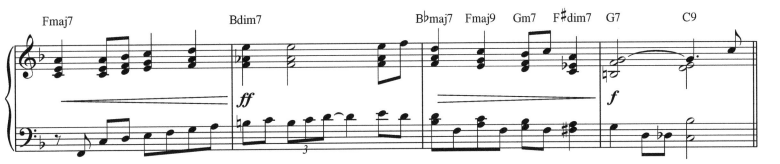

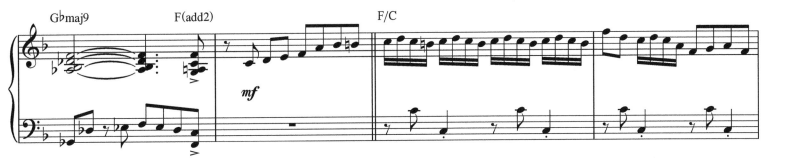

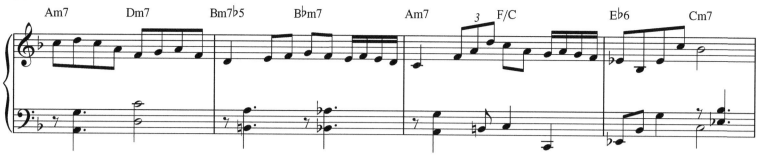

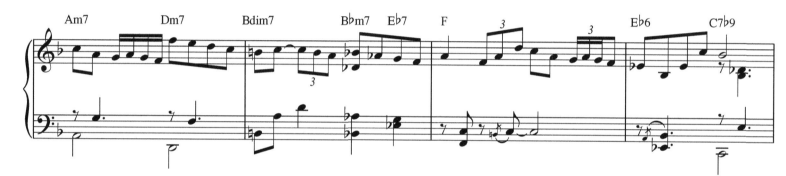

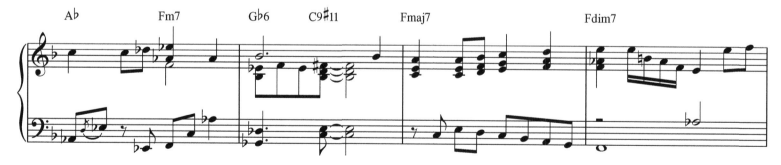

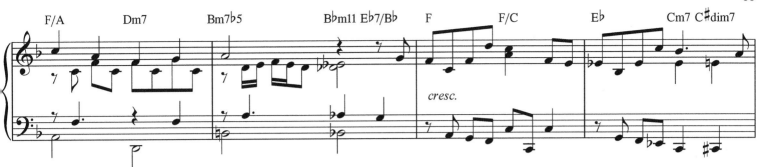

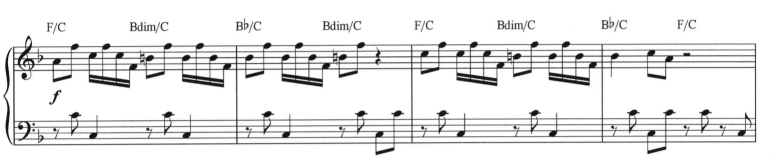

ONCE UPON A TIME
from the Broadway Musical ALL AMERICAN

Lyric by LEE ADAMS
Music by CHARLES STROUSE

Latin groove

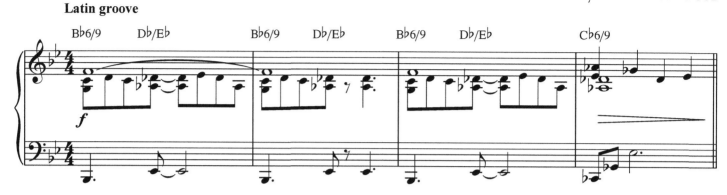

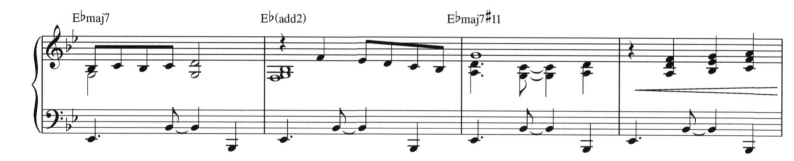

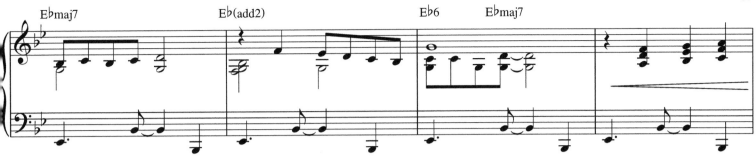

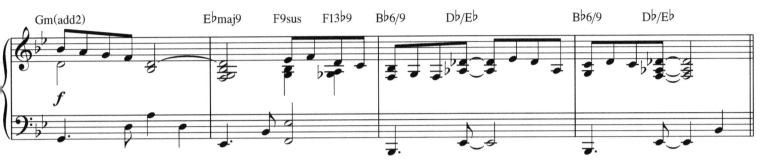

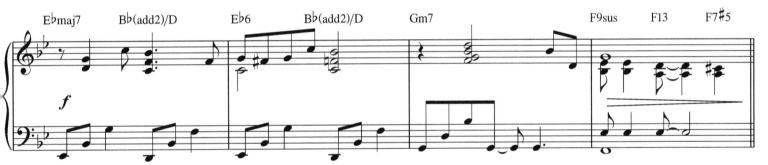

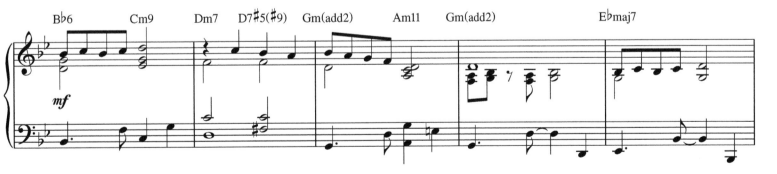

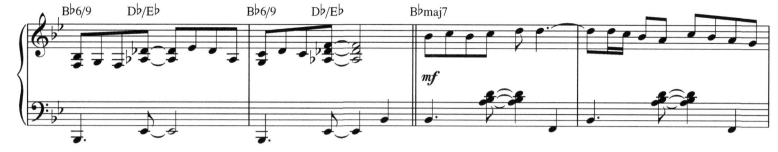

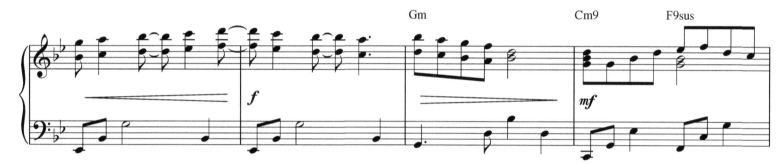

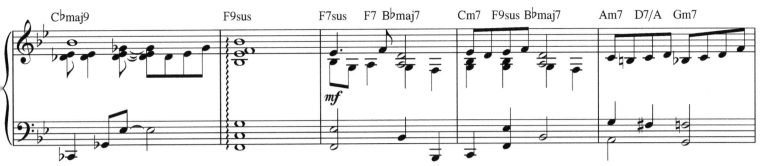

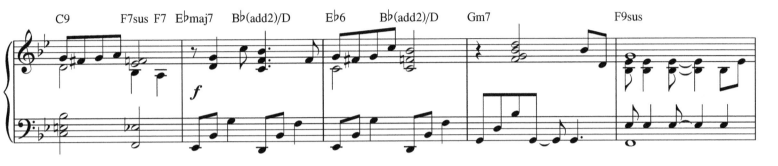

THE SECOND TIME AROUND

from HIGH TIME

Words and Music by SAMMY CAHN
and JAMES VAN HEUSEN

Bright Swing

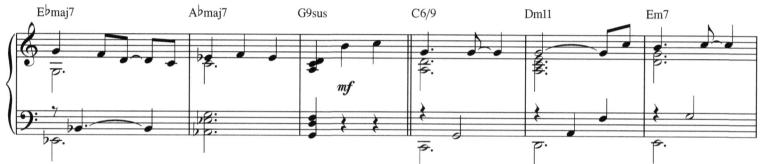

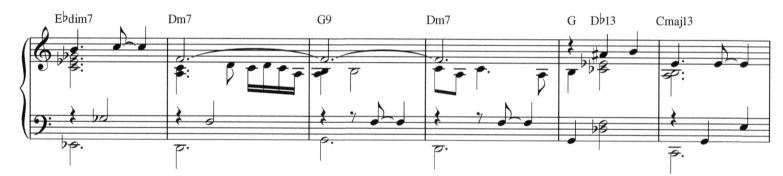

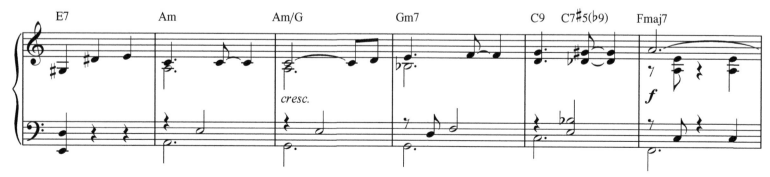

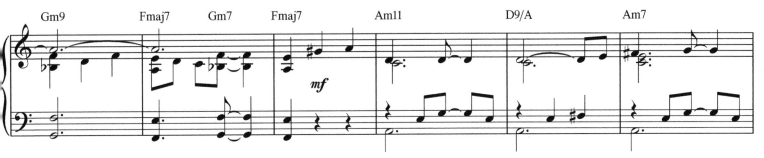

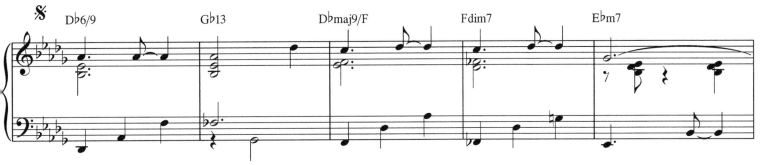

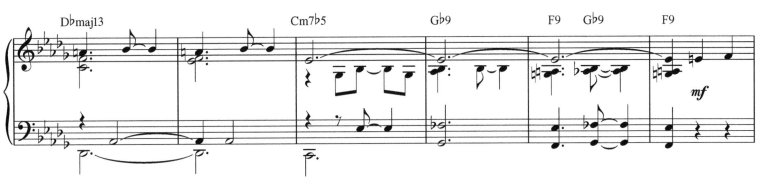

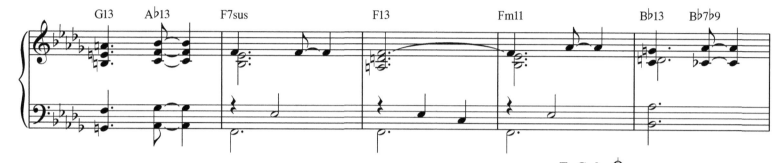

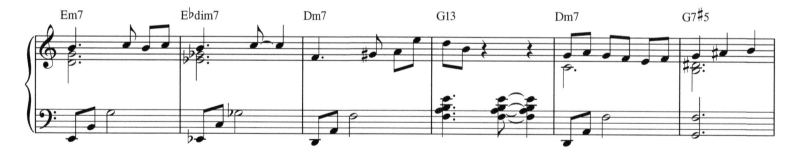

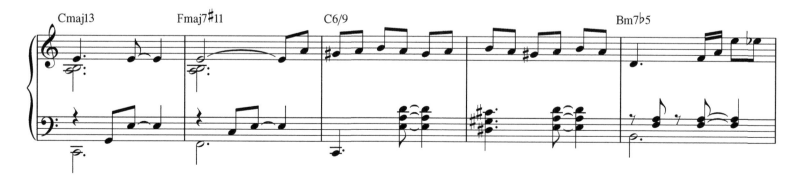

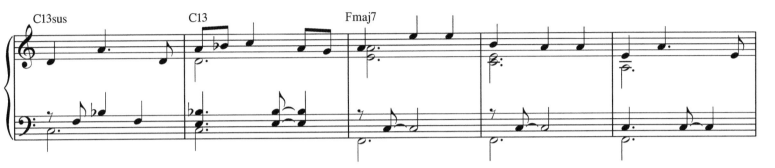

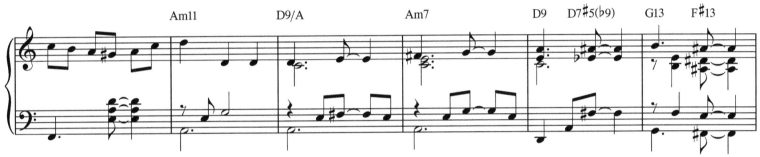

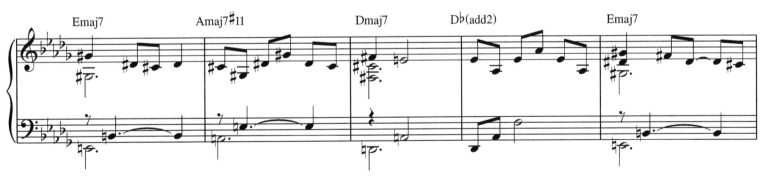

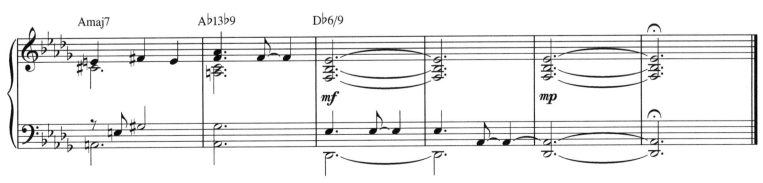

SEPTEMBER SONG
from the Musical Play KNICKERBOCKER HOLIDAY

Words by MAXWELL ANDERSON
Music by KURT WEILL

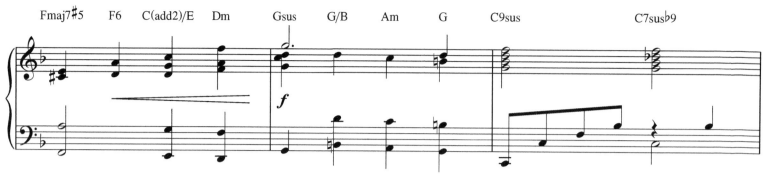

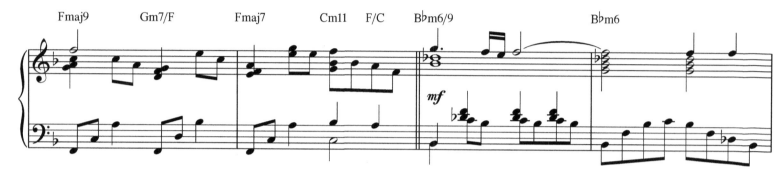

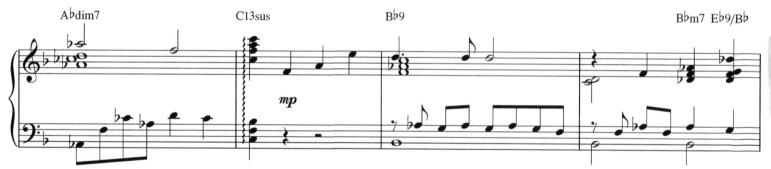

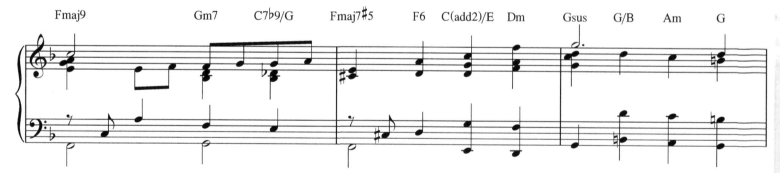